POEMS
for
PEOPLE OF ALL AGES

POEMS

for

PEOPLE OF ALL AGES

LEONARD A. SLADE, JR.

XULON PRESS

Xulon Press
2301 Lucien Way #415
Maitland, FL 32751
407.339.4217
www.xulonpress.com

Printed in the United States of America.

ISBN-13: 9781545619247

To George Hendrick

Contents

"Come grow old with me, the best is yet to be."
—Robert Browning

Supporters

After publicity about my poetry readings
in newspapers and magazines,
I was confident friends would be present
to be cheerleaders for beautiful words.
We began the program with
the faithful few who
listened with respect.
Wine gave us encouragement,
not to mention delicious soul food.
I saw them smiling
as ideas energized attendees
who said that they would
begin reading poetry again
and reaching for the effulgent moon.

My poems! All painful memories, tears, and sorrow!

My poems! All painful memories, tears, and sorrow!
And somehow they keep me writing
About possible beauty somewhere in the world
Maybe in the woods where deer roam.
This walk – I wish I could find flowers
In winter, or any season
To rescue me from self-pity
Yet I know better than
To weep as if I did not have God
In my life to guide me daily.
I am His child – and I
Depend on Him for strength
To keep taking my journeys
In life where He leads me.
O Darling my words have you
I dare not complain anymore.

Morning

Nothing is louder than a buzzard
except a bulldozer
moving the old house
sounds falling to the ground.

Summer Flowers

Flowers, why don't you bloom forever?
      what are you?
On a hot day in July
I admired your colors – red, white, blue
Dancing with grace and style,
Welcoming sun and rain,
Growing with a silence of beauty,
      a silence of time.
Flowers, tell me your secrets.

The Sad Adult

Past, stay behind him,
the night once cried,
the fighting physical
between husband and wife.

Has the heart healed
from the childhood years
and the dark secret
buried now risen from the grave?

Be Like the Flower

Be like the flower, which
Blossoming on dark days
Stands erect with pride
Withstands the heavy rain
Yet opens
Knowing it has beauty.

Lilacs in Spring

He sucked a thumb in Kentucky,
where his father chopped wood
for warm evenings
in December. He wore old
clothes and walked barefoot
among lilacs in spring. And everywhere
he moved, Indiana and Illinois,
laughter filled the air
as young boys teased his height
and demeaned his clothes. No
child ever praised him,
and he for his suffering honored
her, all children thought small
of his future, except her
who read her *Bible* and loved him
as no other person could.
He studied by candlelight,
savoring words and defining dreams
for America. He was hungry for truth
and debated the pros and cons
of slavery. He promised a united country
but blood would taint freedom.
Brother against brother
sister against sister
blacks against whites
Northerners against Southerners –
they all fought for their cause.
Our father of freedom
bathed America with hope
and then was bathed himself
in cold blood.
Children cried.

Rain

**The rain kisses
a cold tin roof.**

**It tinkles making
music and magic
as mother and child
alone hug the night.**

In Frost Valley

Sounds, so clean, so robust,
Energy, so creative, so plentiful,
Teens hug stars
And kiss the moon
For musical ecstasy.

Cat

Among animals
and humans
I love the cat black
in a lap
on a cold
day
lying
still
eyes closed
to crackling fire
and golden flames
free.

Theo

what speed could
anything
exceed than

a schnauzer
swift and docile
chasing

the ball
for
master and child

Robert Lewis (Our Samoyed)

Ghost-like with red devil eyes,
He moves like lightning
Through dancing trees
Breaking deep darkness
Daring the rolling thunder to
Beat him home.

Pure Light

In the evening were the glowing
moon and shining stars, a gift
moving the world. Brighter
now, rays of light,
glimmer of hope; unborn child
on a donkey sleeping in darkness.
We were falling in
Eden, Virgin Mother.
We were waiting on edge
for a new world, for centuries:
praying for you to give birth to
new love and pure light.

Jazz After Dinner

On a snowy evening I shall feel his sounds,
Quietly moaning, inviting cold air to listen,
Call pleasure from golden keys. Old friends
Will kiss their company, sit to relax and dream.
And music, crying, like an elderly man
That sometime after sunrise greets morning
Will pervade the world, profusely fill
That evening and me, celebrating life.

Why I Will Not Be a Child Again

My demons hide
like ghosts after dark:
there is no fear
of light. I will curse
like them the rest
of my life, even
beyond the grave.
Childhood memories make
a hell for adult goodness.
I am lonely in church.
I am eccentric at home.

It is winter.
I feel cold.
I see my child
sleigh riding,
cutting acres of snow.
I am the river.
I am the mountain.
I am the forest.

My soul catches fire –
I am the sun.
I am the moon.
I am a morning star.

Molly

She struts the fields sunrise to sunset
Pulling the plow that cuts black soil. I
Hold the handles as sweat falls,
And pull her ropes right and left.
She huffs and puffs and pulls.
Five years old, I run and follow
Now stop to rub her nose and ears,
Her breath bad and hot with foam.
I lead her to water where
She thinks and drinks
To fill her belly to relieve the pain.
Molly my friend my pet my all
Proudly plows deep and long
Then leans to Mother Earth
To taste delicious worms.

Thank You, Abe!

Abraham Lincoln set me free,
Gave me dignity for the world to see.
Some have said he did not care
About my blackness and the slavery affair.
But I sincerely and honestly believe
This man was called to help us breathe
Truth, righteousness, justice, and all.
America now stands proud and tall.
Thank you, Abe, for what you have done
For giving us victory that's almost won.

The Lombardy Poplar

The majestic poplar tree
taller than the house
last year produced
abundant beauty. But how
proud of limbs confronted
by wild winter winds?
Though strong it may be
there is no guarantee of long life.
Therefore water it often
and feed it with love
before the rites of spring.

Music on My Radio at 5 A.M.

Softly, by the fireplace, Bach is performing for me;
Taking me back to college days, when I was required
To listen to classical music on Saturday afternoons
And fulfill Music 101 requirements, taking notes on Mozart

And Beethoven at 5 A.M., the violin crying for love
And attention wakes Viotti from the grave, his
heart now beats
To the old Saturday afternoon music in college, with
snow outside
And notes in the air, the radio announcer my guide.

So now I wait for Handel to lift my soul
With the great arias of the past. The music
Of college days wakes me, my body is responding
In the depth of remembrance, I pray on my knees
      to be worthy today of this beauty and joy.

"Steep Hill"

**Running up the steep hill
his legs slowed down...
The downpour of rain**

The Red Bicycle

I want to ride
      my red bicycle
so I can exercise
      for longevity.
What good am I
      dead
when I can delay
      peddling
my way
      to Heaven?

The Day My Wife's Dog Cried

When Howard glided out of his kennel,
And the veterinarian waited for his appointment,
I studied his sad face, his glassy eyes staring at me.

My wife rocked and gently rubbed him,
His tears wetted his velvet hair.
His eyes closed forever to greet the stars.

Driving in the Dark

The car moved slowly
Cutting through darkness
Bathing itself with heavy fog.
Red and orange lights
Blinked as warning signals
That danger waited ahead.
The driver prayed for
Bright lights for visibility.
He kept moving slowly
Feeling his way home.

Don't Know Why

Sometimes I cry and don't know why,
Sometimes I laugh and almost die.
Then I cry and cry and cry.
Being Black is going to make me die.

Mendacity

He told us that he did not
Send out holiday cards in December.
When he was thanked for his
Card by his college president
Friend a year later,
When others heard the conversation,
He was embarrassed that
He had engaged in mendacity.
"Don't forget to send us a card
Next year," we politely requested.
He licked out his tongue
And drove his Mercedes Benz
To the liquor store for wine.
Before getting in bed
He fell on his knees,
Asking God to forgive him
For all his iniquities
And to teach him how
To pray and live the Word.

They Kept Driving

They kept driving from one city
To another through rain and snow,
They kept driving around tornadoes
Speeding on highways and dirt roads,
Anxious to reach their destination.
They kept driving their fine automobiles
Their Cadillacs and Jaguars
Until they reached
Their relative's funeral
On time.

Budget Cuts

On the streets, in
hospitals
destitute
they're there – poor
as beggars, ashamed
as misers but visible
more and more –
asking the politicians
Why?
You can see their eyes
absorbing pain now
closing
and morticians
bringing caskets
for rest.

I Fly Away

Sometimes
after church service,
I talk to white folk
My black suit is so dapper.
My wide straw hat
fights the hot sun
while I sip lemonade
and laugh
with blacks and whites
savoring social intercourse
under a Maple tree.
I am cool, cool, so cool.
Then Miss Manners points
to my "fly" in public,
asking,
"What's that you've got there?"
Half my shirt rests outside my pants.
I quickly pull my shirt
inside the proper place.
Laughter from the crowd
accompanies my embarrassment.
Miss Manners is secure now,
having bruised an ego,
evoked laughter, and
tasted power.
She turns red with her smile
and walks away
with her other half.
I strut in the opposite direction,
black and beautiful and proud
of what she did not know.

This Was a Man

This man was the first Black American
to earn a doctorate from Harvard University,
an intellectual giant who interpreted Black

culture; he was born in the North, taught in
the South – enlightened the poor, instructing
the destitute. He studied the meaning of progress

and gave us books and journals and the NAACP; he wrote
sorrow songs of the oppressed, lifted the burdens
of the downtrodden. He inspired talented Blacks

(lawyers and doctors, preachers and teachers,
business professionals and community leaders),
changing a human race. Education was his

weapon for the struggle of equality, for the
taste of justice. He proved Blacks proud
and beautiful, regal and strong. Our

souls are rooted in his whole being, bitter and sweet,
hard and long suffering. He dreamed of
freedom. This was a man, W.E.B.

One Million Black Men's March

In this powerful city Washington, D.C.,
I see Black men holding hands,
And purple gums hollering for freedom
And Black leaders singing songs
Dreaming of brotherhood.

All the proud fathers celebrate solidarity,
Their women stay home to watch,
Honoring their heroes.

Reborn
These Black men grow more beautiful
At the end of the day
And return home cutting darkness
Hoping for love.

1996

Strangers

We mingled with liquid
fermented grapes.
(Bacchus praised us!)
Bread was our body.
We laughed.
Our words spread
like gardens.
water, fresh.
They nurtured growth
between strangers.
black and white.

That made the difference.

Celebrate

Black History
Every month
Of the year
And stretch your
Mind before
Another Revolution
Comes!

Calling All Black Men

Calling all Black men
Real
Responsible
Rich in love.

All Black men
Eligible
for Black women

To love
and
Hold
Forever.

Calling all Black men
Come on
Home Now!

The Street Man

In New York City I saw a ragged man limp
Around Rockefeller Plaza.
I sat admiring red roses.
He hunted soda cans and crumbs
In trash barrels to feed garbage bags.
Curious,
I watched him depart,
The American Flag waving.

Black and Beautiful

I am African-American,
Poet of my people,
Black and beautiful,
Sweeter than chocolate candy
Lover of my queen,
Father of my child,
Conscious of my heritage,
Feet tired and hurting,
Attacked because I'm African,
Rejected because I'm Black,
Despised because I'm proud.
But I smile.
I am Black.
I am beautiful.
I am bad.
Just look at me.

Brown Portrait

A young brown woman
in classy clothes

Her walk stately
in the bread store

The worker ignoring
her presence

Her money ready to spend. Looking
intently at the waitress

She requests bountiful bread
to take with her

The hunger for respect satisfied.

Sounds

I still hear the sounds of slaves
    crying on ships
I hear the master's whip cutting black flesh
    for obedience in the hot cotton fields;
I hear John Brown planning a rebellion
    at Harpers Ferry;
I hear Nat Turner's shots killing white
    Americans in West Virginia;
I hear Henry David Thoreau protesting
    slavery and refusing to pay his taxes;
I hear Abraham Lincoln groaning from a
    gunshot to the head at the Ford Theatre;
I hear Harriet Tubman and Sojourner Truth
    running to church to celebrate freedom;
I hear Martin Luther King, Jr., speaking,
    "I'm free at last, I'm free at last.
    Thank God Almighty, I'm free at last."

I Am a Black Man

I am a Black man
my history written with blood
some sweet songs of sorrow
are composed for my soul
and I
can be seen plowing in the fields
Can be heard
humming
in the night

I saw my grandfather coming to America
and I reached back in time
to help him settle in North Carolina
Leaving England forever

and heard his children cry
for freedom with his last
dime. . . he

gave his African queen twelve seeds
of promise planted deep before
slavery ended. . . and I
promised him honor and freedom

I am a Black man
proud as a Lombardy poplar
stronger than granddaddy's roots
defying place
and time
and history
    crucified
        alive
           immortal

Look at me and be
healed

Elizabeth Keckley

I see Elizabeth Keckley working
As a seamstress for Abraham Lincoln,
Mary Todd being comforted by her,
A former slave suffering floggings,
Now sewing warm red clothes
For the restless First Lady.
Her mahogany body gracing
The White House, her voice sweet
With love in her heart,
She teaches the President
The beauty of Blackness,
the power of brotherhood.
I see a warrior,
I see a modiste,
I see a Saint
Singing in Heaven.

The Black Man Speaks of Rivers, Part 2:

A Tribute to Langston Hughes

'I've known rivers':
'I've known rivers' current 'as the world.'

'My soul grows deep like the rivers.'

I listened to Stokely Carmichael
      When furious fire heated cool air.
I shook hands with Martin Luther King, Jr.,
      Before garbage cans in Memphis.
I heard shots in Dallas
      when John F. Kennedy waved at me.

'I've known rivers.'

I heard the drums of stomachs in New York
      when welfare queens paraded the streets.
I danced to the melody of Diana Ross
      when Leontyne Price sang at the Met.
I read Sunday school lessons at home
      when Alice Walker wrote *The Color Purple.*

'I've known rivers.'

I bathed the body of a Rolls Royce
      when shacks cuddled me with love.
I plowed through books at Morehouse College
      when white men perused works at Harvard.
I moved into the mainstream
      a century after Huck and Jim journeyed down the
      Mississippi.

'My soul grows deep like the rivers.'

The Whipping Song

The Cardinal at my window
sings blood in my veins.
I will tell anyone who asks,
it's made my heart leap, for
who can resist songs at morning?
His clothes burn the Celestial
sun. His quickness arouses
dull senses. If I stare in
his eyes, I am his slave, yielding
to his beauty, whipped by his song.

There Will Be Blacks in Heaven

There will be blacks to teach
what others don't know.

There will be Cleopatra who will
smile as she removes her crown for sleep
on a moving cloud.

There will be Haile Selassie whose
beard will be combed by angels
adoring him.

There will be William Wells Brown who will be
revising his novel, *Clotel*, for the making
of a movie among the stars.

There will be Harriet Tubman chatting
with Abe Lincoln about the condition
of blacks back home in 1993, defining
their oppression, injustice, and mental slavery.

There will be Booker T. Washington debating
W.E.B. Du Bois on the progress of blacks
and the value of integration and segregation
in the South during the good old days.

There will be Mary McLeod Bethune advising
Franklin Delano Roosevelt to speak to Bill Clinton
about the value of historically black colleges.

There will be Martin Luther King, Jr., in front
of Malcolm X, shouting to throngs,
"Free at last!
Free at last!
Thank God Almighty,
Free at last!"

The Black Hair

I have just combed woolly hair,
     Nappy and black,
     Refusing to cooperate,
     Resisting stiff grease,
     Kinky,
     Sensitive,
     Curly.
Why, beautiful hair, are you defiant?
And why are you not free?

Working on the Farm in 1947

On the farm he learned
at five-years-old the mule's
obedience to pull while
he took short steps to
hold the plow steady
and follow.
It was the post-war years
for the world but his father
had land which needed
breaking.

Black people were farming
everywhere in the South
where cotton was king.
Even in the woods, their land,
they dynamited stumps clearing
the way for planting.
In winter weather he skipped school
to pick cotton from sharp bolls –
trembled with cold, a sign of
weakness he was told.

December 24th was Santa Claus time
in their white house on a hill,
nine children in bed warmed their
bodies, hearts beating with fear.
When morning came one bicycle and
one doll baby hugged the Christmas
tree waiting to surprise everyone.

He the eldest rode the bicycle first
down the hill from home was told,
"Don't ride too far. It's dangerous!"
So he rode slowly down the path
and lost control riding himself into

the cotton patch
Falling.

Up again he rode back home the hill
hard to climb.
Falling again. Cotton fields watched
and waited.

The sun went down.
Morning. Cotton acres greeted him.
Another day of cotton picking.
Another day to dream of school.
The doll baby cried.

Mandela

Steel
Hard-boned.
Logic-minded.

He has the universe on his shoulders.
We admire. We see a man.
The man making us safe and protecting our world
and giving us tomorrows.

And with quiet strength and a lion's courage
Mandela imprisoned and demanding
freedom for us.

He sacrifices —
his years and life
for our flesh and blood.

Blackberries, Chocolate Cake and Vanilla Ice Cream in America

I have tasted freedom and
picked blackberries with
Huckleberry Finn. I drank
water from the Mississippi.
I accompanied Abe Lincoln
to the Ford Theatre.
Across the street I sipped
wine and ate bread.
I dreamed of the 13th
and 14th Amendments
satisfying my hunger
and of a U.S. President quenching
my thirst for freedom.
I am still hungry.

Hard Boss
(Inspired by Langston Hughes)

I went to my boss.
Said I have no money.
Went to my boss,
Said I have no money.
My boss said, Colleague,
Can't you just be my sweet honey?

I cried in her office,
She refused to hear me.
Cried in her office,
She refused to hear me.
A man's tears she said
Will never change pretty me.

I wish I had looks to
Persuade like the movie star.
Wish I had looks to
Persuade like the movie star.
I'd kiss her at the drive-in theatre
In the back seat of my car.

The Black Madonna

picking cotton on
a cold day blisters
decorated her black fingers
in the fields

She crawled on her knees
until the sun bowed
to her. Eight children
planted beneath the stars
The earth felt good to her.

You can see her now
a parched face and folded hands
she kneels in a different place
drinking blood and eating bread
at the altar

Comforted
white gloves feel good to her
waving to touch the sky
hymns fill the air
They feel good to her
They feel good to her

Trayvon Martin

They're arguing
because they're afraid
of a guilty or not guilty verdict.

They're fearful
of the death of a prince,
because they lie
when they say he brought

it on himself.
What do they understand?

Do they fear truth
(justice)
which makes neighborhoods
frightened?

They want to believe
he's alive –

but sob.

They want to forgive
but can't.

He looked down
from Heaven

his tears flooded
streets

destroyed bridges
drowned white bodies.

The jurors
hide

unsure
of themselves
dissatisfied
"like the rainbow
colored bird
gone blind
that has light
that sheds not."

Question to a Teenager

I had to bite my
tongue when you disrespected
your mother with venom spewing

and I vomited when I saw you
lick out your nasty tongue at her
and later shouted obscenities

and your mother cried uncontrollably
when you yelled and then left for the beach
on your black motorcycle on Sunday.

How did you drown, neighbor?

Be Careful

Be careful how you treat your neighbor
In meetings or on the street,
For who knows when the mind may snap
And the victim may pull a weapon
To shoot the verbally abusive destroyer.
Assaulting one personally can
Prove to be devastating
For families and communities
And the criminal justice system.
Be careful how you treat your neighbor,
For death can end it all.

The Video Store

The store had DVD's and videos that
He wanted to supplement his teaching,
Except the section that had nothing
But trashy and salacious works.
He paused thinking the sign had
Publicized wholesome videos and DVD's
With content scholarly and uplifting.
His cataracts prevented him
From seeing fine print below the sign.
The store polluted his mind with shock.
He left with a broken heart
And with a diminished spirit
Never to return again.

Toys

Children love looking
under Christmas trees
for doll babies,
BB guns, tricycles,
and many more things
to make them laugh
and cry with happiness.

Street Ticket

The officer came at 4 a.m.
To ticket an automobile
Parked in front of the owner's house.
It would be fifteen dollars
Or face the judge for appeal.
The Town Hall received the
Check with mild protest
Because two other cars
Parked on the street received nothing.
Is it my color, I asked.
The officer who explained
That the ticketing officer
Could have had an emergency
Call after ticketing my
Automobile. Days later
Two cars parked on the
Street between 2 a.m., too.
They would be ticketed
Because of a friendly telephone
Call to the Police Department.
Democracy can work with help.

I Pause Observing Jealous Adversaries

to see their frowns. No matter where they
go, I am still a man.
I'll always anger them with published books.
I shine for my personal God
who wants my good works visible.
Nothing can keep them from cursing me out.
I'll absorb the pain.
And for the future there's a
grave waiting for them
but for now
There's a heaven waiting for me
right here on earth where
I'll savor living experiences and
smell adversaries rotting
in their graves.

Lesson Remembered

I learned how to pray
from my religious father.
He prayed passionately from
his heart at annual revivals
until he died at 93.
"The communication is between
you and God," he taught me.

He sang in the choir behind
the pulpit until he volunteered
prayer at one annual revival.
During the revival the preacher rose
to tell him after his prayer that he did not know
how to pray and critiqued him.
"I was not talking to you;
I was talking to the Lord,"
he said loudly and repeatedly
until the preacher's criticism ceased.
The preacher left church with
his butt whipped and his sermon forgotten.

Albany, New York

They lived and worked in Albany,
New York, where the Roosevelts
and Cuomos had been
governor, where William
Kennedy and Toni Morrison
had taught literature, where Herman
Melville had published masterpieces,
where Presidents Truman,
Clinton, and Obama had
visited, where regional colleges and
universities ranked high,
where health quality
was excellent,
where Bishops and
a U.S. President
were buried,
where citizens remain models for emulation,
and where good triumphs over evil.

Children Love

Children love Moms and Dads
who spend time with them
going to see good movies,
swimming with them at beaches
and feeding seagulls,
and eating cotton candy
and playing fun games
and hugging the new puppy
under the Christmas tree,
going to church or synagogue,
eating meals together
and sharing stories
at the table and
reviewing activities of the day.
Children love Moms and Dads
who tell them daily,
"I love you."

What It's Like to be a Black Professor

First, it's Heaven and Hell and
absorbing pain daily, like being
tortured for the good you're doing,
like celebrating when right triumphs,
it's loving everyone and trusting no one,
meeting beautiful colleagues, friendly
and ugly bastards who forget those
who have helped them professionally,
and dealing with persons who gain
weight sitting, not lifting a finger
to earn their salaries, but wasting
time socializing with visitors, it's
finding beauty and truth, good and
bad in and outside classrooms, and
forgiving your enemies but not for-
getting their names, it's sharing goals
and objectives, wearing clean clothes
and smelling good, and starting on
time and ending on time, not watching
the clock before departure time, it's
fire and fervor and the academy re-
warding faculty and students for
excellence, it's finally being grateful
for the gift to lead and serve in the
best place in the world
before saying goodbye.

What Some College Students Told Me

That I was too hard as a professor.
That they did not know why
      they should know grammar.
That they do not read newspapers.
That it is better to cheat
      than to repeat.
That I should have been a preacher.
That I loved to hear myself talk.
That I graded too hard.
That some students were afraid of me.
That I was one of the meanest
      professors they've ever had.
That some students were stabbing
      me in the back.
That some faculty members
      were jealous of me.
That some administrators see
      me as a threat.
That they wish they had a
      husband like me.
That I should have been
      a college president.
That I was no John Keats
      as a writer.
That I use the power of
      the pen to get my enemies.
That I know how to forgive
      but I do not forget.
That I am more loyal
      to people than they are to me.
That I work too hard.
That I am generous to a fault
That I want more
      for my students than
      they want for themselves.
That I love teaching.

Fifty Years of Matrimony

You accepted my brave telephone calls
when I tried to court you for marriage.
We flew kites together and rode bicycles
and you stopped to kiss me to
tell me "I love you."
Your black hair was long
when I used my nervous hands to comb it.
Your eyes met mine like stars
yielding to the bloody moon.
We would have good times
and bad times living and loving
producing a precious Princess
who would cement the three of us.
She had her cross to bear
at an early age but
God kept her close to Him
while He healed you of
your breast cancer and brain tumor.
You kept driving your red car
to your good church where
your pastor prayed for your
continued healing.
I suffered later not
knowing whether I would live
or die. God intervened
and healed me, too,
to be with you a bit
longer. He was our miracle doctor.
Princess stood by us
both as she directed children's
music at her school reminding

us all that love
conquers pain
and sorrow and suffering.
We sat together yearly at South Beach
at Martha's Vineyard,
where twenty-five years
of visits replenished
our spirits and sustained
us and healed us.
Our love for fifty years conquered all.

Problem

I want to teach
      standard English
so I can teach
      ignorant people
about the language
      being beautiful.
What good is my
      work if
people don't study
      the language
but instead read nothing
      but trash
polluting their minds
      and remaining
pathetic intellectual
      midgets?

Unwinding After Fifty Years in the Classroom

The fiftieth year of teaching
I reflected on the joyous days
and the sad days I succeeded
and failed during the short years
and long years determined to
rebuild a troubled world
by imparting my modicum of
knowledge with students and
inspiring them to become scholars
and leaders and builders
pushing them to give their best
before they visit Bacchus
for wine to celebrate the
love of learning.
We shared a toast
after their commencement
before my benediction.

First Love

He loved his teenage friend
more than any girl he
thought he would ever love
until she told him that
she did not love him.
He confided in his dad
that he was heartbroken.
His dad told him that a new
girlfriend would find him
and keep him forever.
He married his new girlfriend
at the cemetery
and lived with her in three states for
sixty years. He died suddenly
two days before she
succumbed.
They returned to the cemetery happy.

Readers in Church

Readers in church
Walk to the Eagle
The <u>Bible</u> rests precariously
On the podium.

Half of the stand had a hole
Lectors fear moving it
Right or left so that
They could read in a modicum of light.

The lamp had died
For some time now
And the electrical outlet
Took the blame.

And the minister on his side
Had a bright lamp
Perfect to see the Word
For him to preach.

Not until the <u>Bible</u> fell
Through the hole on the reader's side
And he caught it
Proceeding to read with grace

Then the congregation noticed
That darkness could become light
When God communicates
Fix what is wrong in His church.

the yellow airplane

the yellow airplane
moved slowly for takeoff
until it ascended in air
smoothly gliding through clouds
descending an hour later
breaking speed on concrete
finally stopping for deplaning

No Substitute for the Divine

He came from Heaven
to heal me when I was sick.
He gave me money when
I was penniless.
He gave me comfort
when I was sad.
He destroyed my enemies
when I was persecuted.
He spoke to me when
people used me for personal gain.
He promoted me when hypocrites
tried to subjugate me.
He forgave me when I
sinned against Him.
He gave me His power
when I was powerless.
He gave me His cup to drink
His blood when my tears
became Heavenly showers for my soul.

The Country Preacher's Folk Prayer

Eternal God,
We come this mornin'
with bowed heads and humble hearts.

    Uh hum.

We thank you for sparing us another day
by letting your angels watch over our
bedside while we slumbered and slept.

    Uh hum.

We come to you without any form or fashion:
just as we are without one plea.

    Uh hum.

You blessed us when we didn't deserve it.
When we traveled down the road of sin,
you snatched us, and made us taste of the
blood of Thy Lamb.

    Yes, Lord!

This mornin', touch every human heart.
Transform tears into Heavenly showers
for the salvation of sinful souls.

    Yassir.

Remember the sick, the afflicted,
the heavy laden.
Open the windows of Thy Heavenly home.
Let perpetual light sine on them in the
midnight hour.

    Yes Lord.

When we have done all that we can do down here,
take us into Thy Kingdom, where the sun never sets,
where there's no more bigotry, hypocrisy, backbiting;
no more weeping and wailing, before Thy throne, where
you will wipe away our tears; where we can see our
mothers;

I want my mama!

Where, in that city, where the streets are paved in gold and
adorned with every jewel,
where we can see Jesus, sitting on the throne
of glory.

Ummmm mmmmmm a hummmmmm

When we get home, when we get home,
when we get home,

we'll rest in Thy bosom
and praise you forever.

Amen

Acknowledgments

The author thankfully acknowledges the editors of the following works where some of these poems appeared:

Memories for Posterity: "The Yellow Airplane," "No Substitute for the Divine," "Readers," "What It's Like to Be a Black Professor," "Supporters," "My Poems! All Painful Memories"

Jazz After Dinner: "Jazz After Dinner," "Sounds," "I Am a Black Man," "Be Like the Flowers," "Brown Portrait," "Lilacs in Spring," "Black and Beautiful," "The Street Man," "Rain," "A Country Preacher's Folk Prayer"

Pure Light: "Pure Light," "Calling All Black Men," "One Million Black Men's March," "I Fly Away," "This Was a Man," "Budget Cuts," "Why I Will Not Be a Child Again," "Molly"

Lilacs In Spring: "Thank You, Abe," "The Lombardy Poplar," "Music on My Radio at 5 A.M.," "Steep Hill," "Don't Know Why"

Neglecting the Flowers: "Summer Flowers," "Celebrate," "The Day My Wife's Dog Cried"

Sweet Solitude: "A Black Man Speaks of Rivers," "The Whipping Song," "The Black Hair," "There Will Be Blacks in Heaven," "I Fly Away," "Working on the Farm in 1947"

I Fly Like a Bird: "Mandela"

Nobody Knows: "The Hater," "Boss"

Vintage: "Strangers," "Cat"

Another Black Voice: "Blackberries, Chocolate Cake, and Vanilla Ice Cream"

Chasing the Wind: "Hard Boss"

Elisabeth: "The Black Madonna," "Elizabeth Keckley," "Morning," "Theo"

God Put a Rainbow in the Sky: "Trayvon Marten"

The Whipping Song: "In Frost Valley"

I am grateful to Roberta Hall Slade, my wife, for her encouragement over the years. She shared me with Classic Shed, my outdoor study, and with Martha's Vineyard, where many of these poems were written. Thanks also to Marcy Casavant for typing my manuscripts.

My deep gratitude to George Hendrick, my mentor for forty-seven years. His constructive criticism continues to help me grow personally and professionally.

L EONARD A. SLADE, JR., a native of Conway, North Carolina, has lived in Albany, New York, since 1988. He is Professor of Africana Studies, Adjunct Professor of English, Collins Fellow, and Citizen Academic Laureate at the University at Albany (SUNY). He is the Past Director of the Humanistic Studies Doctoral Program and the Master of Arts in Liberal Studies Program. Slade is the author of twenty-four books, including nineteen books of poetry. Slade has received a number of national awards for his work. He studied poetry with Pulitzer Prize Winners Stephen Dunn and Donald Justice.

CPSIA information can be obtained
at www.ICGtesting.com
Printed in the USA
FFHW011702311218
50007828-54737FF